FIRST
PEOPLES
of NORTH
AMERICA

THE PEOPLE AND CULTURE OF THE
APACHE

Cavendish
Square

New York

RAYMOND BIAL

Published in 2016 by Cavendish Square Publishing, LLC
243 5th Avenue, Suite 136, New York, NY 10016

Library of Congress Cataloging-in-Publication Data

Bial, Raymond.
The people and culture of the Apache / Raymond Bial.
pages cm. — (First peoples of North America)
Includes bibliographical references and index.
ISBN 978-1-5026-1010-2 (hardcover) ISBN 978-1-5026-1011-9 (ebook)
1. Apache Indians—History—Juvenile literature.
2. Apache Indians—Social life and customs—Juvenile literature. I. Title.
E99.A6B53 2016
979.004'9725—dc23

2015023310

Editorial Director: David McNamara
Editor: Kristen Susienka
Copy Editor: Nathan Heidelberger
Art Director: Jeffrey Talbot
Designer: Amy Greenan
Senior Production Manager: Jennifer Ryder-Talbot
Production Editor: Renni Johnson
Photo Research: J8 Media

ACKNOWLEDGMENTS

This book would not have been possible without the assistance of a number of organizations and individuals, including many Native people, who have devoted themselves to sustaining the traditions and enriching the contemporary life of the Apache in Arizona, New Mexico, and Oklahoma. I am especially indebted to the staff of the Apache Culture Center at Fort Apache for their gracious assistance. I would like to express my appreciation to the people of the Fort Apache Reservation for allowing me to take photographs there, along with the staff at Native Seeds/SEARCH in Tucson.

I would like to thank the people at Cavendish Square Publishing for their hard work with *The People and Culture of the Apache* and other titles in the First Peoples of North America series. Finally, I would like to express my deepest appreciation to my wife, Linda, and my children Anna, Sarah, and Luke for their cheerful support.

CONTENTS

A young Apache girl shows off traditional dress, circa 1903.

AUTHOR'S NOTE

At the dawn of the twentieth century, Native Americans were thought to be a vanishing race. However, despite four hundred years of warfare, deprivation, and disease, Native Americans have persevered. Countless thousands have lost their lives, but over the course of this century and the last, the populations of Native tribes have grown tremendously. Even as America's First People struggle to adapt to modern Western life, they have also kept the flame of their traditions alive—the languages, religions, stories, and the everyday ways of life. An exhilarating renaissance in Native American culture is now sweeping the continent from coast to coast.

The First Peoples of North America books depict the social and cultural life of the major nations, from the early history of Native peoples in North America to their present-day struggles for survival and dignity. Historical and contemporary photographs of traditional subjects, as well as period illustrations, are blended throughout each book so that readers may gain a sense of family life in a tipi, a hogan, or a longhouse.

No single book can comprehensively portray the intricate and varied lifeways of an entire tribe, or nation. I only hope that young people will come away with a deeper appreciation for the rich tapestry of Native American culture—both then and now—and a keen desire to learn more about these first Americans.

This image shows an Apache member named Go-Shona in ceremonial dress.

CHAPTER ONE

Everyone has a story.

—Veronica Tiller,
Jicarilla Apache

A CULTURE BEGINS

Orth America was not always heavily populated. Many millennia ago, people crossed a frozen landmass through the Bering Strait, which stretched from Russia to North America. The people who migrated into North America spread out and established communities across its vast lands. One of these communities was the ancestor of today's Apache (uh-PATCH-ee) Nation. The Apache are part of an ancient Native American culture that has continued into present times. Today, they have become a well-established group, divided into many different tribes across southwestern North America, with a rich and varied past.

The Creation of the Apache

Each of the Apache tribes has a rich and intricate system of beliefs expressed through stories of the

The Apache called the rugged and arid landscape of the American Southwest home for many centuries.

creation of Earth and the appearance of the first humans. There are many versions of the story, but in each, the Apache emerged from a mystical underworld and came to live in the Southwest. To this day, the Apache remain closely bound to this dry landscape of high mountains, jagged hills, and deep **canyons**, as well as sprawling deserts and dense forests of pine, cottonwood, juniper, and oak.

Here is a version of the story of how the world and the **Jicarilla** (HE-kuh-REE-yuh) Apache, a band that now lives in New Mexico, were created:

In the beginning, there was nothing—no ground, no earth, only darkness, water, and cyclones. There were no people, no living things, only the **Hactcin** (hasht-sheen), or holy people, who have been here forever. It was a lonely place. So, the Hactcin made the earth in the form of a living woman and called her Mother. They made the sky in the form of a man and called him Father.

The Hactcin lived in the underworld. The mountains had a Hactcin as a guardian spirit, as did each plant and fruit that came to grow there. Everything was perfect and holy in the underworld. The people of the underworld were not yet real, with flesh and blood. They lived as if in a dream; they were only shadows of themselves.

One day, the Black Hactcin, who was the most powerful, decided to create the animals. As the people watched, he fashioned a clay figure with four legs and a tail. The figure looked strange to them—until it began to walk. The people were amazed.

The Black Hactcin spoke to the clay figure, "You are all alone, which is not good. I will have others come from your body." With his

great power, the Black Hactcin caused all sorts of animals of the land to emerge from the body of the creature. Even the Black Hactcin was amazed at the great variety of animals, each with its own distinctive appearance and habits. The Jicarilla still delight in these animals that walk or fly about the earth—some with hair, horns, and hooves, others with scales.

The People and Culture of the Apache

The Apache enjoyed endless expanses of desert and sky as their homeland. The landscape of Fajada Butte at Chaco Canyon in New Mexico is shown here.

At that time, all the animals could speak the Jicarilla language, and they asked the Black Hactcin where they should make their home. He told them to spread across the land—the mountains, deserts, and plains—and to live in the place that best suited their nature.

After he had created the animals of the land, the Black Hactcin held out his hand and

In addition to deserts, the scenery surrounding Apachería included mountains, meadows, and low grasslands.

asked for water. A drop of rain fell into his open palm. He mixed the drop with earth and shaped a bird from the mud. "Now use those wings to fly," he said.

The mud figure instantly came to life and flew through the sky, but soon the bird became lonely. He flew in each of the four directions—east, south, west, and north—then came back and told the Black Hactcin, "I can find no other birds."

So, the Black Hactcin whirled the bird around and around. The bird glimpsed many images flashing past him—hawks, eagles, songbirds. These blurred pictures then turned into living birds, which circled the sky. To this day, birds prefer the air, seldom lighting upon the ground, because that first drop of water came from the sky.

The birds then came to the Black Hactcin and asked, "Where shall we live? Where shall we rest?"

The Black Hactcin told them to fly in all directions and then come back to tell him which place they liked best. "You may have that place as your home."

"What should we eat?" the birds next asked.

The Black Hactcin raised his hand east, south, west, and north, and all kinds of seeds fell upon the ground. When the birds went to eat them, the seeds turned into worms, grasshoppers, and many other insects.

The Black Hactcin then told Turkey, "You will be in charge of all these seeds." And this is why the Jicarilla honor this bird's feathers, placing one in each corner of their fields when they plant their crops. The turkey is also striped like Indian corn with a head like a corn tassel. In fact, every part of the turkey's body represents some part of the corn plant.

The Black Hactcin next took moss from the river's edge, rolling it in his hands. When he threw the moss into the water, it turned into fish, frogs, and all the other creatures that

Turkeys are important animals to the Apache and feature in many stories, including the creation story.

live in the water. When the birds flew over the river, some of their feathers dropped into the water and turned into ducks, herons, cranes, and other water birds.

Now the animals and birds had everything, or so the Black Hactcin thought. But the creatures came together in council and told the powerful spirit, "We need another companion. We need people."

"Why do you need others?" the Black Hactcin asked.

"Because you will not always be with us. You will go away from time to time."

The Black Hactcin agreed. "Perhaps someday I will go to a place where you will not see me."

He asked the animals and birds to gather materials from nature, including corn pollen and precious stones. He then instructed them to remain a short distance away from him as he turned to the east, south, west, and north. With corn pollen, he next traced an outline on the ground, just like his own body. He placed the precious stones within the figure and they became flesh and bone—veins of turquoise, blood of red ocher, bones of white rock, bone marrow of white clay, skin of coral, eyes of abalone, pupils of jet, and fingernails and teeth of opal.

The Black Hactcin blew wind into the man and he came to life, the path of the wind marked in the whorls of his fingertips. Noisily pushing forward, the birds and animals were eager to see the man.

The Black Hactcin then instructed the man how to stand up, walk, and run, as well as how to speak, laugh, and shout. When the birds first glimpsed the man, they were so happy they sang as though it were dawn. To this day, at the girl's puberty rite, a man runs in four clockwise circles, as he was once directed by the Black Hactcin, and an old woman makes a chirping noise in her ear.

The man was able to speak with the animals and birds, but otherwise he was alone. So the animals and birds asked the Black Hactcin to help the man. That night the man's eyes became heavy, and he fell asleep. He dreamed long and deep about a young woman, and when he awoke she was sitting beside him.

"Let us speak together," the man suggested. And they did. Then they walked and ran, laughing together. The birds made sweet music so the couple would continue to be happy together.

And this is how the earth and all its creatures and the first two people came to be.

Like other Native peoples of North America, the ancestors of the Apache were hunters and gatherers who made their way across the Bering Strait over a narrow land bridge that joined Asia and North America thousands of years ago. It may have been twelve thousand years ago, but some scientists now think that Asian people first migrated to North America between twenty-eight thousand and thirty-eight thousand years ago. The Apache ancestors, known as the **Athapascans**, are believed to be one of the last groups to cross this land bridge during the last ice age. For thousands of years they lived in an area that is now Alaska and the Canadian Northwest, speaking the same Athapascan language as the other tribes living there. Dressed in animal skins, they hunted mammoths and giant bison, along with deer and other small animals.

Sometime after 1000 CE, most likely between the thirteenth and sixteenth centuries, Apachean people migrated southward along the eastern slopes of the Rocky Mountains into the American Southwest. At that time, the climate of the Southwest was cooler and wetter than it is today, and the land was covered with vast grasslands and lines of trees along the riverbeds. The people adapted to their new world and formed a deep bond with the land that provided them with food, clothing, and shelter. They ate game and wild plants, and they learned where to find water, stones suitable for weapons and tools, and wood for their fires.

Much of the Apachean past remains a mystery. Why, after thousands of years in the cold North, did they abandon their snowshoes and travel all the way to the Southwest? Are their homes, called **wickiups** (WIK-ee-ups), based on the small huts made by Northwest Peoples? Why are the Apacheans of the Southwest so far removed from their Athapascan relatives in Canada and Alaska?

It is believed that most of the Apacheans came in a large, single migration to an area near Gobernador Canyon in northwest New Mexico. Apache stories of origin place their emergence around this area. Small bands of hunters and their families followed over the next several generations.

At the time of their migration, the Southwest was home to several flourishing Native civilizations, including the Anasazi and the Hohokam. It was once thought that the Apacheans drove these peoples from their homes. However, when the Apachean people arrived in the **Four Corners** region, they most likely found that the Anasazi had already relocated to villages in the upper Rio Grande valley in present-day New Mexico. The Hohokam of southern Arizona had also abandoned their ancestral settlements. Today the descendants of the Anasazi are known as the Pueblo, and the inheritors of the Hohokam territory are the Tohono O'odham (also called Papago) and the Pima.

Later, as their way of life changed, the Apacheans drifted into two distinct groups: the Apache and the Navajo. The Navajo settled as farmers in the Four Corners area while the restless Apache spread over three desert regions—the Great Basin, Sonoran, and Chihuahuan. Over time, they scattered farther into what are now southeastern Colorado, Arizona, central and south Texas, and northern Mexico. The word Apache probably came from the **Zuñi** word *Apachu*, meaning "enemy." However, the Apache refer to themselves as **Ndee** (in-DAY), which in their language means "people."

Hardy and clever, the Apache thrived in the Southwest. They made weapons and tools from wood and stone. While the men hunted, the women gathered berries, nuts, and seeds. Whatever they needed they learned to make with their own hands. Artful raiders as well as able warriors, the Apache plundered the storehouses of the neighboring Pueblos, who grew corn, beans, and squash. Although they occasionally traded with the Pueblos, the Apache did not enjoy good relations with their neighbors and, unlike the Navajo, were not heavily influenced by the Pueblos. Although relative newcomers to the Southwest, they were well established in their new home country long before the Spanish, Mexicans, and Anglo-Americans ventured into the region.

Never united as a single nation, the Apache preferred to live in scattered bands, sometimes fighting with each other. Over the generations, they drifted into several

The People and Culture of the Apache

tribes, which came to speak their own dialects, and many smaller groups. In addition to the Navajos, the principal Apachean-speaking peoples came to be the **Chiricahua**, Jicarilla, Lipan, **Mescalero**, and **Western Apache**. The Chiricahua were divided into three bands: the Central and Southern bands, and the Eastern band, whose range joined that of the Mescalero. The Jicarilla were given their name by the Spanish because of their basket-making skills. Mescaleros, or "mescal makers," were so named because mescal from the century plant was the band's favorite food. The Lipan Apache made their home in Texas, while the Western Apache divided into distinctive groups: Northern Tonto, Southern Tonto, Cibecue, White Mountain, and San Carlos. There is also a small band of Yavapai (YAV-uh-pie) Apache in western Arizona.

When they first encountered people of European descent, the Apache were wandering the rugged landscape of eastern Arizona, New Mexico, western Oklahoma and Texas, southeastern Colorado, and western Kansas, as well as parts of Mexico. Those who lived in the eastern portion of this territory, at the edges of the Great Plains—the Jicarilla, Mescalero, Lipan, and Kiowa-Apache—adopted the lifeways of the Plains Peoples. They became skilled horsemen, lived in tipis, and hunted buffalo, while the Chiricahua and Western Apache continued as hunters and gatherers. From the Pueblo, they also learned how to grow corn and melons, and later pumpkins, beans, and squash.

Skillful warriors and raiders, the Apache were feared by the Pueblo and the Spanish and Anglo settlers who crossed their territory. Viewing the Spanish and Anglos as intruders, the Apache

This map shows the Four Corners area of the United States: Utah, Colorado, Arizona, and New Mexico.

courageously resisted having their lands taken away, even after New Mexico was annexed by the United States in 1846. Heroic leaders such as Cochise and Geronimo, both of whom were Chiricahua Apache, battled US forces for several decades.

The Apache and the Landscape

The vast deserts and mountain ranges of the Apache homeland are known as **Apachería**. This region stretches from south Texas to central Arizona, and from northern Mexico to the High Plains of eastern Colorado. When the Apache acquired horses sometime after 1620, bands began to spread over the plains east of the Guadalupe Mountains in southern New Mexico and southwestern Texas. This was a land of brittle grass and small rugged trees called mesquite. Here, the Apache followed the enormous herds of buffalo. About 1718, they were defeated by the Comanches and withdrew to the western edges of the dry grasslands. Some Apache bands joined with the Kiowa in the central plains near the confluence of the Platte and Missouri Rivers and became known as the Kiowa-Apache. They settled far from the Spanish but later found themselves directly in the path of American settlers pushing westward. Other Apache, who came to be known as the Lipan Apache, remained in Texas, where they continued to hunt buffalo and live in tipis.

The Jicarilla Apache eventually moved to the mountainous regions of present-day northern New Mexico near the Rio Grande. The Mescalero Apache ranged in the desert country of New Mexico, south of Jicarilla territory as far as El Paso del Norte on the lower Rio Grande. Here, they battled for survival in a hot climate and rocky, parched terrain. They traded with the Spanish or raided their villages until about 1775 when they finally entered into a peace agreement. Serving as scouts and living among the Spanish, they soon learned their language and adopted many of their customs and clothing styles.

The Apache who lived in Arizona included the Western Apache and the Chiricahua, who historically wandered the seemingly endless stretches of desert in the southeastern part of the state. Here, the Chiricahuas made their way along arroyos, or gullies, followed the trails of deer and small wild pigs known as javelina, and climbed the forested mountains that rose abruptly from the desert floor. This land was laced with canyons and marked by unusual rock formations. Unlike many wandering peoples who were forced to live on marginal lands, the Apache chose to roam the rugged mountains and deserts because they loved this land and their nomadic way of life. This was a place of jackrabbits and coyotes, lizards and snakes, as well as numerous varieties of birds, including eagles, hawks, and owls. Every cactus had painful needles, just as rattlesnakes, coiled beneath the rocks, flashed their fangs, and scorpions threatened with their sting.

Suffering hunger and thirst, extreme heat and cold, the Apache battled for survival. In this land of deserts and ancient mountains, they endured the terrain and the climate, going days without water and eating wood rats or lizards when they could find no other food. To the Apache, every stranger was a potential enemy. In the American Southwest and deeper into Mexico, they skillfully eluded both Mexican and US soldiers in their quest to keep the freedom they so deeply cherished.

Farther north, the Western Apache favored a cool climate and wooded mountains. They made their home—and continue to live—in the high **plateau** country of the White Mountains, well above the stately saguaros and other cacti. Here, there were ponderosa pines, deep blue lakes, and aspens shimmering in the breeze, as well as rushing streams and springs of clear water. The Western Apache homeland extended south of the present-day city of Flagstaff, Arizona, along the Verde River, across a ridge called the Mogollon Rim, into the beautiful White Mountains and down through the Salt River canyon all the way to New Mexico. Their range included the Gila River valley and parts of the Salt River canyon to the Santa Catalina Mountains, on to the Pinaleño Mountains, as far south as the tip of the San Pedro River valley in northern Mexico. The Western Apache hunted deer in the forests and meadows and caught beaver along the streams.

To this day, the Apache gather the hearts of agave, or mescal, to bake over hot rocks. They also traditionally ate cactus fruits, acorns, pine nuts, and walnuts, and they raised corn, beans, and other crops. Wherever they lived, the Apache respected the land, plants, and animals that provided them with food, clothing, and shelter. Their keen knowledge and skill enabled them to thrive, even in the face of difficult conditions. Their dedication to the mountains, valleys, deserts, and canyons that surrounded them bound the Apache to the land on a personal and spiritual level and helped them flourish. Today, they remain connected to the land and consider all things sacred. Their histories and legends are integral parts of their culture and way of life.

The Apache lived in homes called wickiups, pictured here.

*While living I want
to live well.*

—Geronimo

BUILDING A
CIVILIZATION

Each new civilization needs food, water, and shelter. These resources are essential to ensuring a strong, lasting presence in a region. The Apache recognized this and so devised ways in which to structure their communities and fill these basic needs. Hunters, gatherers, and occasionally farmers, the people knew the land intimately—where they might find water, where they had previously hidden food, and where they might pick some nourishing berries. The Western Apache planted corn and other crops, but the harvests were not always bountiful, so the men hunted deer, rabbits, turkeys, and other game while the women gathered cactus fruit and acorns.

Housing

Tribes lived in several kinds of houses. The Lipan Apache, Kiowa-Apache, and several Jicarilla bands lived in tipis, like other Plains Peoples. These cone-shaped homes were made of wooden poles lashed together at the top with rawhide and covered with tanned buffalo hides. A few Jicarilla lived in adobe homes like the Pueblos of New Mexico and Arizona. Like the Navajo, other Apache lived in earth-covered dwellings called hogans.

However, most tribes, including the Mescalero, Chiricahua, Western Apache, and many Jicarilla lived in wickiups, small dome-shaped huts covered with brush, thatch, or animal skins. Until the Apache encountered Spanish explorers, Mexican soldiers, and, later, United States forces, they roamed freely within their home territory. Wickiups could be easily constructed wherever they decided to make camp. When they broke camp, the women packed their belongings, and when they set up the next camp, the women built another wickiup.

To make a wickiup, women set mesquite, willow, or cottonwood poles in a circle of shallow holes, bent the tops over, and tied them together with strips of yucca leaf. On this frame they tied bunches of **bear grass** with yucca string, one overlapping the other to shed the rain. During cold or rainy weather, the women covered the frames with animal skins. In later years, the Apache traded for canvas, which they used to waterproof their dwellings.

The women left a small hole in the top to vent the smoke that rose from the fire burning in a shallow pit in the center of the floor. There was also a low doorway, facing toward the rising sun in the east, which the Apache considered the sacred direction. To keep out the wind and cold, women covered the doorway with a skin or blanket. There was no floor, just the hard-packed earth, which the women swept clean. About 7 feet (2.1 meters) tall, wickiups ranged from 8 to 15 feet (2.4 to 4.6 m) in diameter.

Many Apache families still build shelters like this to keep them cool in hot weather, to weave baskets, and sometimes to cook meals.

Family Units

Each wickiup housed the parents and their children. Two married couples rarely lived together in the same dwelling. Camps were made up of several clusters of wickiups, the number depending on how many married daughters were in the band. About twelve to twenty people lived in each band. The Apache have long been very social—one never sees a wickiup standing alone by itself. A man avoided camping alone, which, despite his courage as a hunter and warrior could have been a distressing, if not frightening, experience. The Apache were accustomed to living with their families, and they enjoyed and needed the company of others within the band.

During the warm summers, the family moved outside and lived in a circular brush windbreak. Women also made brush shades, or ramadas. They set posts in the ground in a rectangle, tied branches horizontally to the posts to brace the structure, and then wove twigs and brush into the frame, making a kind of latticework. Under the shade, shielded from the baking sun, women cooked, wove baskets, and did other household chores.

Possessions

Because they moved so often, the Apache had few possessions. Beds were made with pole frames, cushioned with dry grass and perhaps a blanket. Women also had baskets, water jugs, and pounding stones and stone slabs for grinding nuts, seeds, and corn. In later years, they might also have an iron cooking pot, skillet, or dishpan, which they had acquired through trade.

Joining the Community

The Apache loved raiding and warfare, and from an early age boys were taught to be warriors. They learned to remain absolutely silent as they made their way

Apache baskets are intricately designed and expertly crafted.

across the land, raiding villages or avenging a death. Then they would go without sleep as they stood guard all night. They learned to send and read smoke signals. When the boys were about fifteen years old, they were ready for raids and warfare.

From their mothers, girls learned to do household chores, such as cooking and caring for the children. When they came of age, they underwent a puberty rite known as the Sunrise Ceremony. In this joyous event, girls danced for four days to the beat of water drums and songs. They were blessed in sacred rituals and honored for the strength they would need as wives and mothers.

Apache learned to be tough—they often went for long stretches without food or water, walking up to seventy miles a day in the searing heat. Wherever the Apache journeyed, they carried within themselves an abiding respect for the land. This Apache song speaks of their regard for the land:

> *Far on the desert ridges stands the cactus*
> *Lo, the blossoms swaying*
> *To and fro the blossoms swaying, swaying*

Family Ties

The Apache preferred to live independently in small bands. Historically, they had no central tribal government and did not even come together as a tribe for ceremonies, such as the Sun Dance celebrated by many Plains Peoples. Because the arid land could not provide enough food for large groups of people, the Apache lived in scattered bands composed of several extended families, or family clusters, each with its own territory for hunting, gathering, and farming. Among the Western Apache, society was and still is based upon a system of clans rather than families. Every person is born into a clan. Today there are sixty-two different clans.

The Apache were matrilocal, or centered on the mother's home. Throughout their lives,

Here a Mescalero Apache dances during a ceremony.

The People and Culture of the Apache

daughters usually remained with their mother's band. When a couple married, the husband went to live with his bride's family in a nearby wickiup. As with the Navajo, to ensure harmony in the marriage, the Apache husband and mother-in-law did not speak or look at each other. If the couple ever separated or if one of them died, their children remained with the mother's family. The Apache were also matrilineal, meaning family descent was based on the mother's family— except for the Chiricahua, who trace both sides of the family. The wife's grandmother was highly esteemed within the family. She traditionally wielded a great deal of authority.

Living in camps, extended families formed the basis of social and political life among the Apache. These families, which included the older parents, unmarried children, and several married daughters and their families, usually formed four or five households. Each family had a headman who instilled discipline in his group, ensuring that everyone rose early and worked hard. Between two and six families would join together to form a band, based either on blood relations, marriage, or geographic proximity.

Each band had a leader, or chief, who inherited the position or was chosen for his ability to provide for the people through hunting and raiding. The chief lacked authority to punish anyone, so his role was largely advisory. However, social disapproval was a powerful force in maintaining order among the Apache. The difficult terrain and the threat of hunger also bound the people closely together. Cooperation was essential if they were going to survive as they wandered the

landscape of sharp rocks and hot sand. Protection was also essential. It was unsafe for a woman to gather seeds by herself—she might be attacked by an enemy or wild animal. Other work, such as gathering and baking mescal, required many hands. Men rarely hunted alone, in case of an accident or attack. It thus became customary, even essential, for people to work together and share the bounty of the harvest and the hunt—their fate and fortune depended upon the group, not the individual.

No Nation

Among the different bands, the chiefs were considered equal, but some enjoyed more respect due to their bravery as warriors, their skill as raiders, or their spiritual powers. Several times during the year, the chiefs led their bands to a gathering of the groups that journeyed in the same region or were related by marriage, custom, or dialect. These bands viewed themselves as members of the same tribe, but they never united as a nation. Even when faced by the Comanche onslaught, the Apache on the southern plains preferred

This Kiowa-Apache warrior wears ceremonial clothes and displays a Washington medal, as well as a shoulder insignia denoting the rank of lieutenant colonel.

to live and fight separately, which resulted in their being driven into New Mexico. This nomadic way of life also made it nearly impossible for the Spanish, Mexicans, and the United States military to dominate the Apache, however. Because the intruders had to deal with so many elusive, fiercely independent bands, it was difficult to place the Apache under their control. This resistance continued for nearly two hundred years, proof of the Apache's determination to remain governed by no one but their own people.

There were many people, young and old, living in Apache communities.

CHAPTER

THREE

*Nature explained
everything in life for
the Apache people.*

—Mescalero Apache
website

LIFE IN THE APACHE NATION

Over the years of roaming through the United States, Apache tribes developed a distinct lifestyle and societal structure, complete with rituals, ceremonies, and crafts. Their traditions shaped each tribe, providing spiritual and communal guidance.

The Cycle of Life

The Apache people considered all life sacred. As a result, they had many rituals and ceremonies

for different stages of life. Each milestone was celebrated and commemorated differently. These are some of the views the Apache people held on the cycle of life and death.

Starting Life

Among the Western Apache, an expectant mother wore a maternity belt made of the skins of deer, mountain lion, and pronghorn antelope, since these animals were believed to have little difficulty in giving birth. Medicine men traditionally conducted rituals at the time of birth, but, in more recent times, the mother was attended by a midwife. To wash the baby, the midwife squirted it with water she had warmed in her mouth. Then she rubbed the baby dry with grass, moss, or cloth and sprinkled it with cattail pollen. A few days later, a ceremony called a medicine sing was held at which the child was named.

A **cradleboard** was made, usually of pliable willow, oak, ash, or peeled mesquite root, with a hood to protect the baby's head. The wood frame was padded with moss, shredded bark, or strips of cloth. The Apache often said the baby was placed in the cradleboard "amid much sprinkling of pollen and praying to the gods." To amuse the baby and bring

Apache women carried their children in cradleboards (pictured here).

good fortune, small charms such as bags of pollen, squirrel tails, pinecones, or stone arrowheads were hung from the hood. Chiricahua mothers hung badger paws to protect the baby from fear and cholla wood to prevent colds.

Growing Up

From an early age, children were taught to cooperate and contribute to the good of the family and the band. Children were loved and cherished by their parents and everyone else in the band, yet they were expected to be tough and strong. They had to be if they were going to survive the rigors of the Apache way of life.

Every day, even in winter, boys rose well before daybreak and swam in a nearby stream. To harden them against the cold, they sometimes had to roll naked in the snow. Each day, they also ran to the top of a hill and back carrying a mouthful of water to make sure they breathed through their nostrils. Girls also swam and ran to strengthen themselves. Many were as fast and as powerful as the boys. Working beside their mothers and the other women in the camp, girls also learned to work hard without complaint.

From the age of eight or nine, boys were already hunting with bows and arrows, proudly bringing home cottontail rabbits and squirrels. Apache boys were raised to become good hunters and fierce warriors. Both training and games sharpened their wits, made them skilled with weapons, and instilled in them courage, strength, and endurance.

Rites of Passage

When his training was complete, a young man was allowed to go on his first raid. If he proved himself after four raids, he was considered a man and could join the war parties. If he failed, he was scorned by the band. Young men could not marry until they had shown they could provide for their families by taking part in at least four raids. By this time, they were usually between twenty and twenty-five years old. An Apache girl was generally deemed ready for marriage between the ages of fifteen and eighteen, once she could undertake all the household duties expected of a woman.

Marrying

Marriages were usually arranged by the young man's parents, after which the couples courted—although young people sometimes chose their own mate. Unmarried women were carefully watched by their relatives, but young people found a way to meet at ceremonies. When a young man wished to marry, he asked a relative, often an old woman, to approach the

Many Native people married young.

woman's family. If his offer was accepted, the young man presented the woman's family with gifts—horses, blankets, or guns. The bride's family then presented a smaller number of gifts to the groom's family.

The Apache did not have a wedding ceremony. A dwelling was built near the wickiup of the woman's parents, and the young man simply went to live in his new wife's camp. The couple lived in their own wickiup with the doorway facing away from the parent's home, out of respect for the long-standing taboo that a man should never look at or talk to his mother-in-law. It was believed that this practice eliminated the possibility of conflict and ensured harmony between the households. The man was also expected to help support his wife's parents, although he did not neglect his own mother and father.

Do Not Name the Dead

Like the Navajo, the Apache dreaded the ghosts of the dead. They seldom spoke of the deceased, and then only acknowledged, "He is gone." Fearing that they might catch a disease from looking at a dead person or touching his possessions, people promptly buried the dead or placed the body in caves or clefts between rocks. The Western Apache wrapped their dead in blankets, and as a prayer that the dead person might safely journey to Yaa ka'yu, or heaven, they sprinkled ashes and pollen in a circle around the grave.

The family either buried or burned the possessions of the deceased and destroyed his wickiup. They believed the deceased might return for his belongings and bring the "ghost sickness," which meant death for others in the band. Only a few people attended the burial, and afterward they burned their own clothing. The location of the grave was never mentioned, and if one had to speak of a dead relative, the person was referred to as the "one who used to be called …" then adding the deceased's name.

After a death, children's names were changed if the deceased had called them by those names. The band then moved to another camp, and it was forbidden to speak the name of the dead relative.

Getting and Storing Food

The Apache hunted for game and gathered berries and other fruit to survive. When they acquired horses in the late 1600s, the Jicarilla, Kiowa-Apache, Mescalero, and Lipan Apache began to hunt buffalo on horseback like the Plains Peoples. The buffalo quickly became

The Apache eventually used horses to hunt the buffalo and other large animals living nearby.

their primary source of meat, clothing, and shelter. The Western Apache and Chiricahuas—and the Mescaleros when they migrated to New Mexico—hunted many kinds of animals, especially deer, but also pronghorn antelope, elk, and mountain sheep and goats when they could get close enough to shoot them. They also caught and ate small animals, including opossums, wood rats, and cottontail rabbits—but few liked to eat the jackrabbit, whose meat was considered tough and stringy. However, when food was scarce, people survived on just about any creature they could find.

Some tribes hunted wild turkey and quail for food. They captured hawks, eagles, and turkeys for their feathers, which were used in rituals, on arrows, and occasionally in headdresses. Some Apache avoided bears, believing that the spirits of evil people dwelled in them. Others hunted the powerful creatures not only for their flesh and fur but also for grease used in oiling guns and grooming hair. Mountain lions were killed whenever possible, not so much for the meat but because the skins made excellent quivers. Badger, beaver, and otter were also hunted for their fur.

Occasionally, women and children joined in what was called a "surround hunt." Everyone formed a huge circle and walked slowly toward the middle. Cottontails and other small animals were clubbed as they tried to escape the tightening ring. However, the men most often went on hunting journeys in small groups. Before the hunt they fasted because the spirits were said to look favorably on those in need. Deer was their favorite game, and they had to be excellent stalkers, as well as highly skilled with bow and arrow, to approach and bring down these wary animals. Sometimes, they smeared themselves with grease to disguise their odor and wore deer-head masks as they quietly stalked their prey. They never boasted of their skill or brought along baskets for carrying meat back to camp because they believed such arrogance resulted in bad luck. When they made a kill, they respected the animal as a gift of nature—not as an indication of their hunting ability. When they returned to camp, they were expected to share the meat with others. Fresh venison and other meats were roasted over the fire or boiled in various stews. Deer, elk, and buffalo meat was also cut into thin strips, hung over bushes to dry in the sun, then pounded and stored in leather bags.

Through each season, women gathered cactus fruit, century plants, grapes, acorns, pine nuts, mesquite pods, and walnuts, as well as a variety of other berries, seeds, nuts, and roots. During the early spring, the Chiricahua and other Apache tribes gathered the tender green stems of the yucca plant, which they roasted for a day, sun-dried, and stored. Later, the stems would be soaked in water to soften them before they were eaten. Next the Apache harvested the white rootstocks and shoots of tule plants, which they boiled with meat to make a hearty soup. Later in the season, they picked the white blossoms of the narrow-leafed yucca and boiled them with meat or bones. Then long trips were made and camps set up to harvest the century plant, or mescal. In early summer, women harvested the blossoms of locust trees and picked wild onions.

By midsummer, they were collecting seeds and berries, as well as wild grapes. They journeyed to the desert in July to harvest the fruit of the saguaro cactus and collect the bean pods of the locust tree. In late summer, they went into the mountains to gather chokeberries, which they dried and stored, and to dig potatoes, which they stored in caves. Other autumn bounty included screw beans, broadleaf yucca fruit, prickly-pear cactus fruit, and mesquite beans, which were ground into flour for pancakes. There were also plenty of walnuts, piñon nuts, and acorns. The acorns were mixed with deer jerky and fat, then rolled into balls and stored as a kind of pemmican, an emergency food. At the end of the year, women picked the seeds of grasses. The Apache also loved wild honey. The bees were forced out of the hive with smoke, or men laid skins on the ground and shot arrows until chunks of the comb broke off and fell down. The honey was squeezed into leather pouches. During the winter, the Apache generally

RECIPES

FRY BREAD

Today, fry bread is popular among many Native Americans.

INGREDIENTS

4 cups (946.35 milliliters) flour

½ teaspoon (2.5 mL) salt

1 tablespoon (14.8 mL) baking powder

lard or shortening

1½ cups (354.9 mL) lukewarm water

Combine flour, salt, and baking powder. Add water and knead until the dough is soft but not sticky. Shape dough into balls about the size of a small peach. Press the dough balls into patties about ½ inch (1.2 centimeters) thick. Fry the patties one at a time in about 1 inch (2.54 cm) of hot lard or shortening in a heavy pan until brown on both sides. Remove the fry bread, drain on paper towels, and serve hot with honey or jam.

ACORN STEW

With this favorite Apache dish, you might need to use beef instead of elk or deer, and whole wheat instead of acorn flour.

INGREDIENTS

2.5 to 3 pounds (1.1 to 1.4 kilograms) round steak
(elk, deer, or beef) cut into bite-sized pieces
small acorns [enough to make ¾ cup (177.4 mL) of
acorn flour] or ¾ cup (177.4 mL) of wheat flour
salt

Simmer round steak in about one quart (1.41 liters) of water for three hours, or until meat is tender. Salt to taste. Shell and grind acorns into very fine flour until you have about ¾ cup (177.4 mL) of flour—or simply measure ¾ cup (177.4 mL) of wheat flour. Remove the meat from the pot, reserving the broth for later use. Shred the meat and mix with the flour in a large bowl. (Note: Metal utensils or bowls will discolor acorn flour.) Pour hot broth over the mixture, stir thoroughly, and serve in bowls with fry bread.

lived on stored vegetables, fruits, nuts, and meat until mid-spring when they could begin harvesting again.

Mescal from the agave plant was an especially important traditional food not only among the Mescaleros but for nearly all Apache tribes. It remains popular to this day. Harvesting mescal in May and June before the flowers bloomed, women cut the entire head or crown from the center of the plant. To bake the mescal, they built a fire in a pit lined with stones. When the fire had burned down to hot coals, they laid down wet twigs, rushes, and grass, then piled the heads atop the smoking mass and covered them with more wet grass and twigs and a layer of soil. They built another fire over the pit and baked the heads from one to four days to make the sticky and syrupy food with a flavor like molasses. Dried in thin layers, mescal kept for a long time and provided the Apache with tasty, nutritious food during long journeys.

Green corn was boiled or roasted over the fire. The hard kernels of mature corn were ground into a coarse meal that was used to make **pone** and pancakes. The Western Apache also made a kind of beer from corn that they called tulapai.

Many of these foods were cached, or stored, in clay pots, which were hidden in caves or holes in the ground. They were left there until needed during the lean winter or when the band moved on to the next place. When traveling in dangerous territory, women kept food bags and water jars filled in case they had to flee during the night. Individuals also carried small supplies of food attached to a belt.

The Apache roasted, baked, and boiled a wide variety of foods from plants and animals to make breads, soups, stews, and other dishes.

Clothes and Accessories

To make commodities such as jewelry and clothing, women prepared the skins of deer, antelope, elk, and buffalo. If the hair was to be removed, they buried the skin for a few days in moist soil, then soaked it in warm water, stretched it over a pole, and removed it with a dull knife. With a sharp knife, the women next scraped the remaining flesh from the skin, then stretched and dried it in the sun to make a stiff leather called rawhide. To soften the leather, they worked the brains of the animal into the rawhide. After the skin had dried, they rubbed and stretched the leather until it became soft and pliant. Women fashioned rawhide into storage pouches called parfleches and the soft leather into bags, blankets, and clothing.

Men usually wore buckskin breechcloths drawn between the legs and tied around the waist, leaving a flap hanging down in the front and back. They draped buckskin ponchos over their shoulders and wore buckskin leggings and moccasins with rawhide soles to protect their ankles and calves from cacti and jagged rocks. The eastern Apache wore the Plains-style low-cut moccasins while the western tribes turned down their tall moccasins at the knee to make a pocket for carrying knives and other objects. Men usually wore their hair at shoulder length and tied a cloth headband across the forehead.

Traditionally, women wore buckskin skirts, along with ponchos and moccasins like the men. They generally wore their hair long, although unmarried Western Apache women shaped their hair into an hourglass-shaped roll tied with a bow. Both women and men shampooed their hair with aloe. The roots of this plant were collected and pounded into a pulp, placed in water, and worked into a sudsy lather. The hair was then combed with a short bunch of stiff grass tied into a firm bundle.

The Apache obtained cloth and wool from the Pueblos and other tribes. It was not until the early 1900s, however, that most men began to adopt Euro-American styles, including white cotton shirts, cartridge belts, and black vests. During this time, women came to favor long-sleeved cotton blouses and full skirts. The dresses were plain or calico, edged with a wide ruffle at the bottom. In later years, many women also began to wear numerous strands of beads around their necks from which mirrors, shells, bear claws, colored Mexican beans, and other medicine tokens were hung. They also liked earrings made of pieces of iridescent shell from the Pacific coast, as well as brass or silver bracelets.

Today, the Apache continue to wear traditional clothing during ceremonies. During her puberty rite, a girl dons a two-piece buckskin dress of the highest quality. Her fringed dress is adorned with shells, beads, and little pieces of metal. When leading ceremonies, the **shaman**, or medicine man, wears a buckskin garment decorated with feathers, beads, and paint to indicate his spiritual powers.

Arts and Crafts

Along with making wickiups and buckskin clothing, women were highly skilled at many handicrafts, including pottery and basketmaking. They made deerskin storage bags, which they dyed brown with walnut hulls. Gourds were fashioned into cups, while plates, spoons, and awls came from bones and wood. Handmade pots were usually gray or brown with rounded bases and flared rims. These pots did not need to have flat bottoms because they were placed on the sandy ground, not on tabletops. The Apache used the pots as cooking vessels. However, they did not have many pots since they could be easily broken during their travels. Of all their talents, the Apache were most skilled at basket making. Using both coiling and twining, they made many kinds of baskets decorated with geometric and animal designs using vegetable dyes. Light and portable, baskets were used for storage, sifting, and gathering.

Women wove four different types of baskets: trays and bowls, storage jars, carrying or burden baskets, and water jars coated with pitch. The most common were trays and bowls, ranging from 4 to 30 inches (10.2 to 76.2 cm) in diameter and with flared sides. These were used for many tasks—serving and boiling food, holding flour, sifting seeds, crushing berries, and parching corn. Tapering to a small neck with a wide rim, tall jars were used for storing dry goods. These baskets were fashioned by coiling thin cottonwood or willow splints over a base of three peeled branches. Women decorated their baskets and jars with black

Apache women were usually responsible for making baskets, such as this one, in which to store food and water.

geometric designs, which stood out against the tan color of the splints.

The Apache made large burden or carrying baskets from split sumac or willow twigs in a technique called twining. They decorated the wide-mouthed baskets with three or four bold horizontal bands and fringed them with strips of buckskin, or in more recent years, with tin cones or pendants. Water jars were essential in the desert country where water was scarce. The jars could be large or small, with a narrow neck and a leather handle on each side. To make these jars, women wove strips of split sumac. Sometimes they rubbed red ocher over the jar to fill in the spaces in the weave and to create a striking design. Then, with a stick to which they

The People and Culture of the Apache

had attached a scrap of buckskin or a piece of shredded yucca, they coated the inside of the jar, and occasionally the outside, with melted piñon pitch.

Most Apache baskets were similar in shape, but the designs of each tribe could be distinctive. The Jicarilla were known for their small baskets, which served as drinking cups, while the Western Apache made black-and-tan baskets with small coils and a fine, even weave. Both the Chiricahua and Mescalero often used yucca leaves, which gave their baskets a light green or brown color.

Apache men crafted weapons for hunting, raiding, and warfare. They made bows, which were 3 to 4 feet (0.9 to 1.2 m) long, from mulberry, oak, or locust wood. They first cut, smoothed, and seasoned the wood, then bent and tied the bow, which was finally placed in hot ashes. When the bow was removed and cooled, it retained its curved shape. Sometimes, they backed the bow with sinew for added strength. Men painted solid colors on the outer edge and designs on the inside of the curve of the bow. They made the bowstrings from split deer or buffalo sinew twisted into a strong cord. To make arrows, they simply fire-hardened the tips of wooden shafts, although the Western Apache and Chiricahua favored canes or reeds, which they fitted with a hardened foreshaft of mulberry or mountain mahogany.

Men made their own stone points or picked up arrowheads at ancient ruins and tied them to the shafts. About 30 inches (76.2 cm) long, arrows were fletched with the split tail or wing feathers of eagles, buzzards, or red-tailed hawks attached with sinew or piñon pitch. The shafts were then painted with red or black bands. The Apache also made quivers and bow covers from mountain lion hides, including the fur and tail, although deer, pronghorn, and wildcat skins were also used. They also made war clubs, hide shields, and lances with fire-hardened tips, as well as stone knives.

Telling Stories

Apache stories instructed and entertained young and old alike. Held sacred, these stories explained the creation of the universe, the origin of the Apache, and the mysteries of nature. Today, these stories continue to hold importance for the Apache people. They not only connect the people to their ancestry, but also deeply root them in their religious and traditional beliefs and practices. Some stories, such as the adventures of Coyote and Big Owl, amused people while also offering lessons. To the Apache, animals had power and continue to do so in modern times. Coyote was honored as a hero because he taught the Apache how to survive in often harsh terrain in the Southwest. He also showed them how to plant corn, weave baskets, and, most importantly, how to build a strong society. He could be a mischievous character, however, who made foolish decisions and then had to suffer the consequences. In other words, just like people, he had many flaws.

Here is a Chiricahua Apache story about how Coyote brought fire to the world, which the people desperately needed for cooking and keeping warm on cold winter nights:

In the beginning only the birds had fire. They kept the fire in a secret place and would not share it with others.

One day, Coyote wandered to where the birds' children were shooting arrows. He began to play with the little ones beside the bluff, and he quickly won all their arrows in the shooting contest.

"Do you know the path to that bluff? I know the way," he said to the children. He didn't really know how to get there, but he wanted to steal the fire and hoped to trick one of the little birds into telling him how to get to it.

The young birds answered, "Our parents told us not to tell anyone."

"I'll give half these arrows to anyone who can tell me how to get up that bluff," Coyote declared.

Although the little birds wanted their arrows back, they again refused. So, Coyote offered them all the arrows, and the youngest bird blurted, "See that piñon tree on the edge of the bluff? If you tell that piñon to bend down, it will lift you up to the bluff."

Coyote gave half the arrows to the bird. He wanted to make sure he was telling the truth before giving up all of them. He told the piñon tree to bend down, and it did so. Then the tree carried Coyote up to the bluff where the birds made their home. He met the birds and told them he had exciting news. "All your enemies throughout the country have been killed!" he cried. "Let us have a great celebration tonight!"

The birds were delighted with this news. That evening they came together, making four large rings for each of the different kinds of birds.

When no one was looking, Coyote slipped away and stripped off the soft bark of the juniper tree, which he tied under his tail. Then he returned and joined in the dance, making sure he got close to the fire. Every now and then he stuck his tail into the orange and yellow flames as the others were enjoying the celebration.

One of the birds told Coyote, "Old one, you're going to burn your tail."

"Let it burn!" Coyote cried joyously. "I feel so happy that all our enemies have been killed. That is why I am acting this way."

But some of the birds quickly became suspicious. "Friends, he is trying to get away with our fire," they said.

"No, no," Coyote assured them, "I'm just celebrating."

He stuck his tail into the fire one more time, leaving it there long enough for the juniper bark to ignite. Then Coyote ran away into the night.

The birds were not able to catch him, so they begged Wasp and Hawk to make the rain fall. But as the torrents came down upon him, Coyote gave the fire to Bumblebee, who sheltered the flames in a hole in a tree.

After the downpour, Coyote shared the fire with all the creatures of the earth, which is how people acquired fire. The Chiricahua say it is also why Coyote's tail is now scorched yellow underneath and burned black at the tip.

Off to War

During the seventeenth century, bands of Apache raiders roved the land, often sweeping as far south as Jalisco, Mexico. Some Apache, most likely Jicarillas and Mescaleros, traded with the Pueblo people of New Mexico, exchanging hides, tallow, and captives for cotton cloth, tobacco, and food. Instead of trading, however, most Apache, in parties of four to twelve men, preferred to raid Pueblo villages, as well as the camps of other Native peoples. They stole horses, corn, and goods, and they kidnapped women and children. Later, they attacked Spanish, Mexican, and Anglo settlements in a similar fashion.

Although the Apache struck terror in their victims, they viewed raiding simply as a means of providing for themselves, like hunting and gathering. They could have completely destroyed all the villages in the Mexican provinces of Sonora and Chihuahua, but they needed the inhabitants to continue to raise livestock and crops for them to steal. They preferred to quietly slip into villages in the early morning, seize livestock or food, and leave without a trace. Masters of deception, they could seemingly blend into the rocks and brush around them. They often raided a village and vanished before anyone realized what had happened. Then the raiders might ride or run hard, going without sleep for four or five days until they were certain they were not being pursued. They had remarkable strength and endurance—a man on foot could run seventy miles a day. When they arrived back at their camp they were expected to share their plunder with everyone.

An Apache might recite this chant when he wished to hide from his pursuers:

> Right here in the middle of this place
> I am becoming Mirage
> Let them not see me,
> For I am of the sun.

The Apache usually went to war to avenge a wrong—including fighting among themselves. If one Apache killed another, the maternal relatives of the slain were obligated to avenge his death. If a Mexican or Anglo killed an Apache, even if he had been stealing horses, the chief of his band or clan raised a war party against the enemy. War parties might have as many as two hundred men, including a medicine man who predicted the outcome of the conflict.

Everyone who wished to join the war party came together in a going-to-war ceremony. In preparing for battle, they called upon the supernatural, which they referred to as "the enemies against power." They believed this force allowed them to surprise and quickly defeat their foe. It could raise a strong wind and clouds of dust to conceal them or make their horses easy to handle during the attack. The great leader Geronimo and some Apache women also believed that this force gave them the power to know what was happening far away.

On the warpath, the Apache were intent on killing the enemy or any of the enemy's people. If they captured an adult male, he was handed over to the women in the dead Apache's family to be killed. Captured children were usually adopted into the band.

Masters of the surprise attack, the Apache preferred a guerilla style of warfare. With only a few thousand people, including women and children, in each of the divisions, they could not afford to lose many people in pitched battles. They scorned heroics, favoring stealth over open warfare. "I am calling on the sky and earth," warriors chanted. "Bats will fly and turn upside down with me in battle. Black sky will enfold my body and give me protection, and earth will do the same."

The Apache did not let their small numbers discourage them. They were determined to keep their freedom and so resisted all efforts made by larger forces to control them. From the seventeenth century to the nineteenth century, they endured and persisted. It was only through being tracked by their own people that they were all eventually caught and forced onto their allocated reservations.

The Apache lived among sprawling mountains and under painted desert skies.

CHAPTER FOUR

We were once a large people covering these mountains. We lived well. We were at peace.

—Cochise

BELIEFS OF THE APACHE

The Apache are a people with many personal and spiritual beliefs. As discussed in Chapter 3, they believe names have power and do not say the names of deceased loved ones. This is a practice passed down through generations. Today, their spiritual lives are still deeply rooted in tradition.

The Apache thought owls brought many diseases and illnesses to their people.

Spirits

The traditional religion of the Apache includes many divine spirits, the most prominent being White Painted Woman, also known as Changing Woman, and Ussen (sometimes Ysen), the Creator. Among the Apache, the sky, earth, sun, and moon are spirits, as are the Water People and the Mountain Spirits, known to the Western Apache as Gan. The Gan, who inhabit caves hidden in the rocky slopes, once lived as people but became spirits in search of eternal life. Like other Native peoples, the Apache religion was part of daily life. It aided in hunting, gathering, and farming, as well as protected them from injury and illness.

The Apache dreaded any kind of ailment—either physical or spiritual. If a disease struck their camp, they fled in panic. They also believed the worst maladies were borne by creatures, especially owls, bears, and coyotes. Such illnesses had to be treated by a medicine man or woman, called a shaman, who had acquired special powers from these animals. The Apache especially dreaded owls, and the appearance of one of these birds around camp aroused great concern. There were no jokes and few stories about owls because it was considered bad luck to even mention the bird's name.

The Apache greatly feared ghosts and witches as well. Ghosts were believed to be the souls of the dead—most of whom were sinister. They might chase or throw rocks at people, or play other harmless tricks. If ghosts weren't treated properly, they could also bring misfortune and even death. Many people believed that ghosts rose from their graves and entered the bodies of owls. The hoot of an owl was the haunting voice of a ghost making threats against the living. Anyone who heard the words would contract the owl sickness, which was believed to be fatal unless treated by a shaman whose powers came from owls.

Unlike ghosts, witches—or sorcerers among some Apache tribes—were thought to be living people who possessed magical, evil powers. Witches or sorcerers, who could be men or women, worked mostly at night, often allying with evil spirits to harm others. Many Apache believed that all injuries and ills were brought on by their curses. People carried charms, such as turquoise beads, cattail pollen, and eagle feathers, to ward off their evil influences. If they were the object of a witch's malice, they asked a medicine man to hold a special ceremony to cure them.

Medicine men or women had the power to heal both the body and the soul. They relied on songs,

Bears were animals also thought to bring disease to the Apache.

prayers, and sacred objects to remove a witch's spell and to cure the sick of ailments ranging from snakebite to arrow wounds. It was believed that supernatural power came only to those who searched for many years. Only then could one become a medicine man or woman. These shamans were thought to divert evil, foretell the future, and treat spiritual maladies, such as the deadly owl sickness. They also led ceremonies and sacred dances. These rituals, however, required the mastery of many elaborate chants in a language that differed from everyday Apache.

When European settlers arrived in Apache territory and eventually claimed the land, many Apache members eventually converted to Christianity. Today, many Apache people are Christian. However, they also

A Jicanilla Apache chief

continue to believe in the old ways and uphold traditional Apache practices. Many people follow both religions in their communities on reservations in New Mexico and Arizona.

Rituals and Dances

Led by the medicine man or woman, most Apache ceremonies had to do with healing the sick, preventing misfortune, or conducting puberty rites, although they might also be held to bring good fortune in hunting, the cultivation of crops, waging war, or rainmaking.

Among the most important is the Sunrise Ceremony, in which a girl is welcomed into womanhood. It is believed that White Painted Woman, or Changing Woman, initiated this ceremony in ancient times. The ceremony continues today. In it, the girl undergoing this rite is called by the name of this divine spirit during the four days and nights of the ritual and for four days afterward. Some Apache place the young woman in a ritual tipi. She traditionally wears a buckskin dress that has been dyed yellow—the color of sacred corn pollen—and decorated with symbols of the sun and moon.

A young girl (*left*) is attended by a female relative (*right*) while participating in the Sunrise Ceremony.

There are many rituals that make up the Sunrise Ceremony, including the molding ceremony, in which the girl is massaged by a woman attendant— usually a relative—to ensure she grows into a strong and independent young woman. It is also believed that this ceremony will give her a good temperament. Sacred pollen is sprinkled, and the girl must drink through a straw so water does not touch her lips, which might result in the growth of unwanted facial hair. She must use a scratching stick instead of her fingernails to keep her skin unblemished. She also throws a blanket as a symbol of future wealth in each of the four directions, beginning with the east. She must learn all of the dances of her tribe and perform them, sometimes for four to six hours at a time.

On the fourth morning, the ceremony often concludes with a footrace, the throwing of gifts, and the dismantling of the tipi. The girl is also welcomed into womanhood by a painting ceremony, in which her godmother and godfather—very important people in the young woman's life—bless her. Her godfather paints her hair and face with white corn liquid, transforming her into Changing Woman. The young woman can then look forward to good health, prosperity, and a long life. Those who attend the ceremony also share in her blessings. It is believed that during the ceremony and for four days afterward, the young woman also possesses healing powers. Once the ceremony is over, the woman is ready to marry and take her place in society.

There is feasting, dancing, and singing during a Sunrise Ceremony. The medicine man or woman recites long chants and ritually smokes. One of the

A young girl on the San Carlos Reservation is painted with cornmeal as part of the Sunrise Ceremony.

most exciting events is the nightly performance of crown dancers representing the Gan, or Mountain Spirits, whose presence is said to remove negative spirits and bestow blessings on the girl. Four to sixteen dancers, along with a clown, dress in buckskin kilts and paint their entire bodies with black, yellow, and white designs. They wear striking masks with high, arching headdresses and then dance by the light of the fire. Here is a verse of one of the songs offered up by the medicine man as part of the ceremony:

> *In the middle of the Holy Mountain,*
> *In the middle of its body, stands a hut,*
> *Brush-built, for the Black Mountain Spirit.*
> *White lightning flashes in these moccasins;*
> *White lightning streaks in angular path;*
> *I am the lightning flashing and streaking!*
> *This headdress lives; the noise of its pendants*
> *Sounds and is heard!*
> *My song shall encircle these dancers!*

Today, ceremonies such as this remain important to the Apache. In the early 1900s, the American government tried to assimilate Native people into American culture and banned the practice of the Sunrise Ceremony as well as other religious rites of passage. Still, Apache people practiced in secret until 1978, when a religious freedom act focusing on Native Americans was passed, allowing the Native people to once again practice the ways of their tribes openly.

An Apache family sits in front of their summer hut in 1933.

The lives of Native groups changed forever with the arrival of Europeans.

CHAPTER FIVE

I was born on the prairies where the wind blew free and there was nothing to break the light of the sun.

—Geronimo

OVERCOMING HARDSHIPS

The Apache and other Native groups in North America lived relatively undisturbed until the fifteenth century, when European settlers arrived, first on the East Coast, and then later in the Southwest. The appearance of Europeans on Native lands alarmed Native groups and led to centuries-long struggles—the Europeans sought to control more land while the Native groups tried to maintain their independence. Many Native American nations were changed forever.

First Encounters

It is believed that the Zuñi were the first Native people of the Southwest to encounter the Spanish when Franciscan missionary Marcos de Niza arrived in 1539. A year later, the Spanish explorer Francisco Vásquez de Coronado, searching for the legendary Seven Cities of Cíbola, journeyed northward from New Spain (now Mexico and Baja California) with a party of Spaniards and Natives. While visiting the western pueblos, inhabited by the Hopi and the Zuñi, as well as the northern New Mexico pueblos along the Rio Grande, he stole corn and cotton clothing. The party did not find any treasure and returned to Mexico, but the Spanish kept coming back. During their search for gold, the conquistadores took food and supplies from the peaceful inhabitants. If the people refused, they were severely punished or murdered.

Unlike the Pueblos who lived in villages, the Apache avoided the Spanish by moving from place to place. The Jicarillas and Mescaleros were the first Apache to directly encounter the Spanish when they met Francisco Vásquez de Coronado's expedition in western Texas and New Mexico in 1540. It was not until 1598, however, that the Apache were forced to deal with the Spanish intrusion into their territory. In that year, an expedition led by Juan de Oñate came into Pueblo country in the upper Rio Grande valley. There, in present-day New Mexico, Oñate established a Spanish colony. Apache first clashed with the Spanish in 1599 when they helped to defend Acoma Pueblo against an attack by Oñate. By 1610 the town of Santa Fe had

Francisco Vásquez de Coronado makes his way into New Mexico.

been founded, and a few Apache bands, notably the Jicarilla, initially got along with the newcomers.

The Apache quickly learned the value of horses. Until the arrival of the Spanish, their only domesticated animal had been the dog. By trading and raiding, however, they acquired mounts and became expert horsemen. It is believed that by the 1630s Pueblos escaping Spanish enslavement had joined the Apache and taught them how to ride horses. Like the Spanish, Apache used braided ropes of horsehair and rawhide, saddles with wooden frames, stirrups, and cinch rings. For saddle blankets, they relied on deerskins, buffalo robes, or sheepskins.

Four Apache members ride on horseback, circa 1906.

Battles for Survival

Throughout the seventeenth century, the Spanish countered Apache raids on villages and travelers by capturing Apache and selling them into slavery, often sending them south where they worked in mines. Yet the Apache continued their raids, and during this time

no village or road was safe. Herds of sheep, cattle, and livestock vanished in the night, forcing people to abandon entire villages. Apache raids left the cavalry unit at the presidio of Santa Fe horseless, so they couldn't ride after the attackers. Then the Apache, mostly Jicarillas and Mescaleros, as well as some Navajos, joined in the Pueblo Revolt of 1680. Led by the great Pueblo leader Popé, this union of Native Americans drove the Spanish completely out of New Mexico.

However, the Comanches had also acquired horses as they moved southward from present-day Wyoming. Quickly adapting to a plains way of life, they drove the Eastern Apache—the most powerful and feared Native people of the southern plains—from the sprawling grasslands just as the Spanish were reconquering New Mexico in 1692. Settling in eastern New Mexico, where they could no longer hunt buffalo, the Eastern Apache began to alternately trade with and raid the Spanish and other Native peoples of the Southwest.

Conflicts continued with the Spanish for most of the 1700s. When the Spanish entered into a peace treaty with the Comanches in 1786, they engaged Comanche and Navajo warriors as troops to fight along with Spanish soldiers and hunt down the Apache bands. The Spanish promised the Apache provisions if they agreed to settle near missions. Forced to cease their raids, some Apache bands lived peacefully with the Spanish until the Mexican Revolution (1910–1920), while others continued to make life hazardous for anyone who dared to venture into their lands.

When Mexico won independence from Spain in 1821, the Apache came under new, Mexican rulers. Although Mexico then governed the territory, including the present states of Arizona and New Mexico, it did not have enough soldiers to maintain effective control over the Apache. Then, in 1846, the United States declared war on Mexico and quickly took the land that would become the states of New Mexico, Arizona, Utah, Nevada, and California, as well as parts of Colorado and Wyoming. The Apache now found themselves under the authority of the United States government, but they still refused to surrender their homeland.

By the end of the Mexican-American War in 1848, the Apache had returned to raiding and warfare, often attacking Anglo homesteads. Known for their hostility, the Apache viewed these new settlers as intruders in their territory. United States officials, who did not understand the Apache, attempted to conquer the wandering people with brute military force, but the Apache, under the great leaders Cochise and, later, Victorio, refused to be confined to reservations. During the 1870s, they

This statue of Cochise was made by Betty Butts and donated to the Fort Bowie National Historical Site in Arizona in 2004.

resisted every effort to subdue them, as the United States embarked on what turned out to be a lengthy war in which they futilely pursued the Apache. The Apache Wars, as they came to be known, did not end until 1886, when Geronimo and his band finally surrendered and were sent to Florida, far from their ancestral home.

Sadly, at the end of this long conflict, many of the Apache were treated as prisoners of war. Removed from their homeland, they were sent to Alabama and, later, to Florida, where they suffered terribly in the humid climate. During this time, many children attended what was called Indian Industrial School in Carlisle, Pennsylvania, and likewise endured uncomfortable and difficult conditions.

Many people died between 1886 and 1894, when groups of Apache were moved to a reservation at Fort Sill, Oklahoma. Some of the larger Apache groups were later moved from Florida to reservations in New Mexico or Arizona. Today, the Fort Sill Apache people have acquired more land in Oklahoma, as well as part of their original territory in New Mexico and Arizona, but they are still working hard to gain more land and recognition.

The Carlisle Indian Industrial School in Carlisle, Pennsylvania, was known as a place where Native

A classroom of Native children at the Carlisle Indian Industrial School in 1901.

children were sent to learn American customs and traditions in order to be assimilated into American life. Classes were taught only in English. Many schools like this, run by the government and missions, arose in the 1890s. They were just one of the many tactics used to get the Apache and other Native groups to abandon their customs and heritage.

Forced onto reservations, the Apache also suffered from poverty, malnutrition, and diseases, especially tuberculosis. By 1914, nine of every ten Jicarilla people were afflicted with this contagious disease. Between 1900 and 1920, one out of four people died.

One of the reservation schools had to be turned into a tuberculosis sanitarium and was needed to treat patients until 1940.

Citizenship

Like other Native Americans, the Apache were not granted citizenship until 1924. They have since battled for their rights and the restoration of their homelands through legal means. In 1970, the Jicarilla Apache received nearly $10 million in compensation for lands taken from them. Today the Jicarilla Apache live on around 1 million acres (404,685 hectares) of land in northern New Mexico. In the twentieth and twenty-first centuries, tribal leaders have vigorously worked to sustain the history, language, and customs of the Apache, notably through educational and cultural programs. They have also vigorously pursued economic independence and pioneered the Native American casino movement. The tribes are constantly working to promote and celebrate their culture, customs, and history.

Preserving the Language

The Apache languages belong to the Athapascan language family. There are four branches of this language family: Northern Athapascan, Pacific Coast Athapascan, Eyak, and Southwestern Athapascan. Sometimes called Apachean, Southwestern Athapascan includes seven separate though very closely related dialects: Navajo, Western Apache, Chiricahua, Mescalero, Jicarilla, Lipan, and Kiowa-Apache. Although all the dialects vary from one another, they share many words and can be understood by the different groups of Apache.

Apache culture has been preserved through language. In fact, the different Apache groups have continued to speak their native tongue, which is even taught in public schools. You may wish to speak a few words of this fascinating language. They may appear a little difficult, but if you follow this guide, you will gain some understanding of how words are pronounced in the Western Apache dialect.

The following examples are drawn from *Western Apache–English Dictionary* edited by Dorothy Bray in collaboration with the White Mountain Apache Tribe.

The vowels are pronounced as follows:

a   as in *father*,

e   as in *west*

i   as in *police*

o   as in *low*

u   as in *hut*

Double vowels like *aa* are pronounced the same, but the sounds are held a little longer. Some Apache words are nasalized, most of the air being expelled through the nose rather than the mouth, as in *m*, *n*, and *ng* in English. The vowels of these words usually have a hooked accent mark (a reversed, upside-down question mark) under them but are here indicated in **boldface** type. There is also a special kind of *L* intersected by a diagonal line (here in *italics*), which is voiceless, like a puff of air with the tongue in the *L* position. It is pronounced somewhat like the English "slip." The tone mark (') after a syllable means that you raise your voice when you say the syllable. The accent mark over a letter (e.g., í) means that letter is stressed or emphasized, or that it is a glottal stop, as in *k'aa*, which is pronounced something like kuh-AH.

Some of the following words are especially important to Apache people. Others are everyday words.

mansáána	apple
k'aa'ist'aaní	arrow
izis bena'iltiní	bag
bé'ísts'óz	beans
shash	bear
ishkiin	boy
hosh	cactus
hilwozh	canyon
tazhik'áné	chicken
ni' dáá gosgah	desert
gósé	dog
itsá	eagle
iyéézh	egg(s)
shitaa	father (my)
bitaa'	father (his/her)
ko'	fire
chiizh	firewood
lóg	fish

it'een	girl
gozdog	heat
hách'ílgish	lightning
ndeen	man
itsi'	meat
izee	medicine
ké'igan	moccasin
shimaa	mother (my)
baa'	mother (his)
dzil	mountain
bizé'	mouth
dah	no
da'idányú	outdoors
búh	owl
hoshcho	prickly pear fruit
gah	rabbit
ikágé	rawhide
túnlíí'	river
óltag	school
bichagosh'oh	shadow
disis	shirt
kee	shoe(s)
tl'iish	snake
bee ijizhé	snare, trap
shíí	summer
ilch'ígó'aahí	teacher

bikoh	valley
tsinagháí	wagon
gozil	warm (weather)
tú	water
hai	winter
isdzán	woman
aa	yes
igáyé	yucca

Language is just one of the ways that Native nations are trying to preserve their culture and heritage. Each year ceremonies and events occur that connect the Apache and other Native tribes to the rituals and ceremonies of their ancestors. Non-Native groups are likewise recognizing this, with many people participating in and contributing to Native celebrations across the United States.

Despite hardship and turmoil, the Apache and other Native groups continue to survive. They are working to gain more recognition and win back lands that were the territory of their ancestors. Many have also taken to social media to offer services and information about their tribe to other communities around the United States and across the world.

Young and old continue to live as members of the Apache communities today.

CHAPTER SIX

I point to my mind,
I also point to my land.

—Ronnie Lupe,
Chairman of the White
Mountain Apache tribe

THE NATION'S PRESENCE NOW

The Apache people continue to exist today. As of 2015, the Apache are a federally recognized tribe. This status gives them the ability to self-govern and entitles them to certain benefits from the government's Department of Indian Affairs. Having this type of acknowledgment has helped the Apache maintain communities around the United States.

A group of family homes on the San Carlos Reservation, circa 2004

Most Apache live on one of five reservations in the Southwest: three in Arizona and two in New Mexico; however, there are also a few communities in Oklahoma and Texas. Others have moved from the reservations to pursue job or education prospects. The Western Apache make their home on the Fort Apache, Tonto, and San Carlos reservations in east-central Arizona. The Jicarillo and Mescalero Apache live on reservations in New Mexico. The Chiricahua, who ranged in Arizona and New Mexico as well as Mexico, were removed from their own reservation in 1876 and imprisoned in Florida in 1886. Years later, some Chiricahua relocated to Oklahoma, where they still live at the Fort Sill reservation. There are also Kiowa-Apache in Oklahoma and Lipans in Texas.

Adaptability

Over the years, the Apache have proved themselves to be highly adaptable, even as they honor many of their traditional ways of life. When the Jicarilla formed a sovereign tribal government in 1937, most of the first tribal council members were medicine men or other traditional leaders. Many people living on the reservation continue to speak the Jicarilla language and follow Apache religious beliefs. Yet today, fewer children are learning to speak the language of their parents and grandparents, so tribal leaders are using educational programs such as the Jicarilla Apache Department of Education, as well as social media and cultural centers particular to each tribe, to help preserve their cultural heritage over the generations. The language is also preserved through Internet archives and language videos on sites such as YouTube.

Most Apache in Arizona speak English. However, because many parents want their children to learn Apache as well, excellent bilingual programs have been established in the public schools on the San Carlos and Fort Apache Reservations. Schools are helping to provide vocational skills so that tribal members may stay on the reservation and earn a living. Tribal leaders reason that if people can live within the community, Apache culture and social life are more likely to be sustained. Many people now work on farms and ranches, and the Apache have become well known as excellent rodeo competitors. Many men and women have also become teachers, university professors, doctors, and artists, although they often must leave the reservations to pursue these fields.

Making Connections

Today, many Apache tribes have established a firm presence in digital and social media. Many of them have their own websites, which you can find in the Further Information section at the back of this book, and some have dedicated Facebook, Twitter, and Instagram pages. More and more people are connecting to Native tribes through online resources. YouTube, for example, offers a network for Native and non-Native people to come together. Learning tools such as language lessons and documentaries introduce people to the Apache history and way of life. With the aid of these social media platforms, many more individuals can come to better understand and appreciate the Apache and their varied traditions.

Revenue

Cattle, timber, and mining leases have become important sources of revenue on many reservations. A number of business enterprises also thrive on Apache reservations. The San Carlos cattle operation alone generates around a million dollars in sales annually. The Fort Apache Timber Company, owned and managed by the White Mountain Apache in east-central Arizona, had brought in much money for the tribe; however, it closed in 2010 after losing $84 million. It reopened in 2013 as White Mountain Apache Timber Company and is still operating today. Established by an Act of Congress in 1897, with a population of thirteen thousand people, the Fort Apache Reservation also operates a popular ski resort, motel, casino, and restaurant, and it hosts the

Some of the terrain surrounding the San Carlos Reservation is mountainous.

White Mountain Apache Tribal Fair and Rodeo, which celebrated its ninetieth year in 2015. The annual event includes a parade, carnival, night dances, arts and crafts, and traditional sunrise dances.

Tourism, including hunting, fishing, and camping, has also become important to the economies of many reservation communities. Offering such opportunities ensure the Apache remain connected to the land. Having once fought anyone who ventured into their homeland, the Apache now welcome visitors. Like the White Mountain Apache, the Jicarilla and Mescalero Apache operate ski resorts. The Mescalero operate the Inn of the Mountain Gods, a resort with a golf course, horseback riding, tennis, and other recreational

Montezuma Castle National Monument in Arizona.

opportunities. On their small reservation, the Yavapai Apache in Camp Verde, Arizona, run a tourist complex at the Montezuma Castle National Monument.

Lasting Legacy

Traditional crafts, including baskets and pottery, are still being created on many reservations. This artwork illustrates how the Apache legacy lives on in the people of its tribes. Over the centuries that they have lived on North American soil, the Apache and their ancestors have created a civilization that has survived despite hardships and turmoil. By persevering during difficult times and fighting for recognition as one of North America's First Peoples, the Apache have ensured their survival. They have proven that despite setbacks and even bans, they are a people who will not leave their heritage or culture behind but rather will embrace it and celebrate it, whatever the cost.

It is up to younger generations to carry on the traditions of the Apache people.

A young Apache mother looks fondly on her child.

CHAPTER SEVEN

I could never turn away from my history.

—Allan Houser

FACES OF THE APACHE NATION

Within the history of the various Apache tribes there are certain men and women remembered and celebrated for their efforts and achievements. These are some of history's most notable Apache figures:

Alchesay (Alchise) (White Mountain Apache) (active 1870s–1880s) was a sergeant in the Indian Scouts under the command of General George Crook. He took part in the Arizona campaign of 1872–1873 against the Apache and Yavapais. In 1875 he received the Medal of Honor in recognition of his work. In 1886, he also helped Crook track down Geronimo, Chato, Kayatennae, and Mickey Free. Although he cooperated with the United States, he advocated fair treatment of his people. With Chato and Loco, he was a member of a delegation that met with President Grover Cleveland and other government officials. However, the delegates were unable to prevent the exile of the Apache to Florida. Alchesay later became a successful cattle rancher.

Apache Kid (The Kid) (Chiricahua Apache) (circa 1865–ca.1894), army scout and outlaw, served in the US Army under Al Sieber, chief of scouts in military campaigns against Geronimo during the 1880s. Sieber likely dubbed him "The Kid" and newspaper stories about his life as an outlaw later referred to him as "The Apache Kid." In 1887, Sieber left the Apache Kid in charge of the scouts at the San Carlos Agency. In his absence, the Apache Kid and the scouts killed another Apache whom the young man suspected of murdering his father. When he returned, Sieber ordered the arrest of those involved, and a fight ensued. Sieber was wounded in the foot and the Apache Kid, along with several companions, escaped. Several weeks later they surrendered, and the Apache Kid was sentenced to seven years. The small band escaped on their way to prison, however. All were captured or killed, except the Apache Kid, who became one of the most notorious outlaws in Arizona. For years, he attacked settlers, taking their food, and many murders in the territory were attributed to him.

Mickey Free, one of the other Apache scouts, tracked the Apache Kid but never caught up with him. Finally, in 1894, an Apache woman said she had been with the Apache Kid as he lay dying in the mountains, most likely from tuberculosis. In 1897, Free claimed that he had found the remains of the Apache Kid in the mountains of New Mexico.

Chato (Alfred Chata or Chatto) (Chiricahua Apache) (ca. 1860–1934), leader and scout, escaped with Geronimo from the San Carlos Reservation in 1881. They hid out in the Sierra Madre in Mexico for about a year, then returned for several raids. In the early spring of 1883, while Geronimo and Chihuahua searched for livestock in Mexico, Chato led twenty-four warriors into Arizona. They were looking for ammunition and killed at least eleven settlers in several raids before heading back to Mexico. In retaliation, General George Crook attacked Chato's camp in Mexico, but the Apache warrior resisted. He and his band of sixty Apache finally surrendered in February 1884. Geronimo surrendered a month later with his band of eighty Apache.

In 1885, Geronimo fled from the reservation again. The following year, Chato helped General Crook track down Geronimo at Canyon de los Embudos in Mexico. However, in 1886, he also joined a delegation to Washington that demanded that the Apache be allowed to remain in their homeland. Although he had helped the army, Chato was exiled to Florida with Geronimo and the other Apache prisoners. He lost his land and livestock at San Carlos. His children were later taken away from him and sent to the Carlisle Indian Industrial School.

In 1894, Chato, Geronimo, and other Apache exiles were moved to Fort Sill in Indian Territory, near present-day Lawton, Oklahoma. In 1913, he was at long last allowed to return to New Mexico, where he made his home on the Mescalero Reservation. He died many years later in an automobile accident.

Cochise ("Hardwood") (Chiricahua Apache) (ca. 1812–1874), leader, was falsely accused of kidnapping a child—who later grew up to become famed army scout Mickey Free—and rustling cattle from a ranch in 1861. Some three months after the alleged kidnapping, US Army Lieutenant George Bascom led a troop of fifty soldiers to Apache Pass in the heart of the Chiricahua homeland. Setting up camp, Bascom requested a meeting with Cochise, who arrived under a flag of truce with his family, including his son Naiche. Although Cochise insisted he had nothing to do with the matter, Bascom tried to arrest him. Cochise managed to escape, though he was wounded in the scuffle. Bascom held many of the Apache as hostages. In ensuing raids, Cochise also captured several settlers. When negotiations failed, both the Apache and the soldiers executed their hostages.

The **Bascom Affair**, as it came to be known, triggered the Apache Wars. The Mimbreno Apache, under the leadership of Mangas Coloradas (Cochise's father-in-law), and the Coyotero Apache from the White Mountains joined Cochise. Their raids, especially during the Civil War when soldiers no longer manned the region's military posts, nearly drove Mexican and Anglo-American settlers from Arizona. In 1862, three thousand California volunteers were brought in under the command of Colonel James H. Carleton. Cochise and Mangas Coloradas ambushed the troops at Apache Pass. Although the smaller band of Apache held off the soldiers, Mangas Coloradas was wounded in the battle.

The following year, Mangas Coloradas was captured and killed by Carleton's troops, and Cochise became the leader of the Apache warriors. Over the next decade, from a secret hideout called the Stronghold in the Dragoon Mountains of southern Arizona, Cochise and his men swept down on settlers along the Butterfield Trail. Expert at deadly raids and quick escapes, Cochise was feared throughout the territory.

In 1871, Colonel George Crook took command of the army forces in Arizona. With the help of Native scouts, he went after Cochise. After tracking down the famed leader, Crook negotiated a peace agreement, which Cochise rejected when he learned that his band would be sent to a reservation at Fort Tularosa, New Mexico. In the fall of 1872, General Oliver Howard, serving as President Ulysses S. Grant's representative, met with Cochise for eleven days. The general honored Cochise's request to live on a reservation near Apache Pass, and the great chief agreed to keep peace among his people. He remained true to his word until his death in 1874. His oldest son, Taza, who became chief, also kept the peace agreement, but upon Taza's death, Naiche, the younger son of Cochise, allied with Geronimo. By 1876, the Chiricahua Reservation was dissolved, and Apache raiders, led by Victorio and Geronimo, again terrorized the Arizona settlers.

Mangas Coloradas (Mimbreno Apache) (ca. 1797–1863), Apache leader and father-in-law of Cochise, lived in the Mimbres Mountains in southwestern New Mexico. After Mexican officials offered a bounty for Apache scalps and many people were murdered, Mangas Coloradas united several bands under his leadership. They raided until the United States took over New Mexico Territory. In 1846, he signed a peace treaty with General Stephen Watts Kearny. However, conflicts arose over the return of Mexican captives and the murder of an Apache that went unpunished. There were further conflicts when miners passed through the region during the California Gold Rush of 1849. Mangas Coloradas intensified his raids on settlers and travelers along the Butterfield Trail.

In the early 1860s, when soldiers left the forts in Apache country to fight in the Civil War, California governor John Downey sent volunteers to protect the route through Arizona. In 1862, the Chiricahuas under Cochise and the Mimbrenos under Mangas Coloradas attacked the advance column at Apache Pass. Mangas Coloradas was shot in the chest and taken to Mexico where a doctor was ordered to care for him. After he recovered, he continued to raid until General Joseph West sought a meeting with him under a flag of truce. However, when he arrived at the army camp, he was taken prisoner and sent to Fort McLane on the Mimbres River. General West apparently wanted the leader to be killed and two sentinels shot Mangas Coloradas, claiming he had tried to escape.

Upon the death of Mangas Coloradas, Cochise became the principal chief of his band in the Apache Wars.

Dahteste was a beautiful Apache warrior woman.

Dahteste (Chiricahua Apache) (ca. 1860–1955), scout, warrior, and interpreter, was a woman of immense beauty and powerful persuasion. She chose to be a mother, a wife, and a warrior, perfecting weaponry and combat techniques. She was fluent in English and served as interpreter, messenger, and mediator between her people and the US Cavalry. She was instrumental to the surrender of Geronimo to the US government, and served eight years in prison for helping Geronimo during his campaigns. Having survived severe illnesses that killed many Native people while imprisoned, Dahteste was eventually released, and nineteen years later she was allowed to return to her homeland on the Mescalero Reservation in New Mexico. She became a lifelong friend to another woman warrior, Lozen, the sister of Victorio.

Delshay (Tonto Apache) (ca. 1835–1874), leader, agreed that his band would live near Camp McDowell along the Verde River in Arizona and report occasionally to a Native agent there. In 1871, following the massacre of Apache at Camp Grant and an assault on Delshay by a soldier stationed at Camp McDowell, Delshay asked if his band could report to an agency in Sunflower Valley, which was closer to the homeland of the Tonto Apache. However, he received no answer.

A year later, in response to Western Apache raids, General George Crook embarked on the Tonto Basin Campaign. After several grueling battles, the troops surrounded Delshay's band. They surrendered and were taken to Fort Apache on the White Mountain Reservation of the Coyotero Apache. Unhappy with their confinement, Delshay and his band moved from Fort Apache to Fort Verde along the Verde River. They were allowed to remain there as long as they did not attack settlers. They lived peacefully until they were joined by Apache suspected of murdering Lieutenant Jacob Almy on the San Carlos Reservation.

Crook called for the arrest of Delshay, who escaped into the Tonto Basin. For months, he artfully eluded the pursuing soldiers. Finally, Crook placed a bounty on him. In July 1874, an Apache brought in a head that he claimed was Delshay's. However, another Apache also presented what he claimed was Delshay's head. Crook gave rewards to each of the men and displayed one head at Camp Verde and the other at the San Carlos Reservation.

Eskiminzin (Eskaminzin, Hackibanzin, "Angry Men Standing in Line for Him") (Aravaipa-Pinal Apache) (ca. 1825–1895), leader and peace advocate, was born a Pinal Apache, but he married into the Aravaipas and became a leading chief. In 1871, as conflict between Apache and settlers escalated, Eskiminzin met with

Lieutenant Royal Whitman at Camp Grant near Tucson. He requested that his people be allowed to remain in their homeland, where the agave plant was their main food, instead of moving to the White Mountain Reservation.

While Whitman sent the request to his superiors, the Apache set up camp near the post. They planted cornfields, collected agave, and cut hay for the soldiers and settlers. However, raids in the spring of 1871 were blamed on Eskiminzin's band, and a gang of vigilantes under William Ouray attacked and killed about 150 members of Eskiminzin's band, mostly women and children. Outraged by the attack, President Ulysses S. Grant ordered a trial and offered to make peace with the Apache. The vigilantes, however, were acquitted, and the Apache intensified their raids.

Eskiminzin's people peacefully rebuilt their wickiups and replanted their fields. However, in 1873 they were relocated 60 miles (96.5 km) away to the San Carlos Reservation on the Gila River. When Lieutenant Jacob Almy was killed in an uprising of San Carlos Apache the following summer, Eskiminzin was mistakenly accused and arrested by General George Crook. In January 1874, Eskiminzin escaped and led his band off the reservation. Months later, they returned, weary and hungry, and Eskiminzin was briefly jailed.

In 1876, Eskiminzin took part in peace negotiations in Washington, DC. Taza, the son of Cochise and leader of the Chiricahua Apache, died of pneumonia during the journey. He was succeeded by his younger brother, Naiche, who accused Eskiminzin of not taking proper care of Taza. To avoid a confrontation, Eskiminzin moved from the San Carlos Reservation and set up a ranch on the San Pedro River. When the ranch was destroyed by Anglo-Americans, Eskiminzin went back to the reservation. In 1888, he was arrested for simply associating with the Apache Kid, who was married to Eskiminzin's daughter Chita. Eskiminzin was exiled to Florida with Geronimo and his Chiricahua Apache. He was permitted to return to Arizona in 1889.

Mickey Free (Mig-ga-n'-la-iae) (Pinal Apache) (ca. 1847–1915), interpreter, scout, and tracker, was born in Mexico. His mother was Mexican and his father part Irish and part Pinalino. When he was about fourteen years old, he was kidnapped, which helped to trigger the Bascom Affair and the Apache resistance led by Cochise. He may have given himself the name "Mickey Free" to acknowledge his liberation from the Apache.

At age fourteen, after he had been released, Mickey Free rescued the wife of an army captain from an attack by two Mexicans at Fort Bowie, Arizona, killing the men with a knife. When he was twenty, Free became an interpreter and scout in the US Army, under George Stoneman. During the 1870s and 1880s, Free helped to track Geronimo through Arizona, New Mexico, and northern Mexico. During most of his career, Free served under chief of scouts Al Sieber.

He also served as the official interpreter for the Chiricahua on the San Carlos Reservation. In 1886, he traveled to Washington, DC, as interpreter for a delegation that included Chato, Loco, and Alchesay, which sought to prevent the exile of the Apache to Florida. After this time, Free tracked the Apache Kid, as well as many outlaws. He claimed to have found the remains of the Apache Kid in 1897. He retired from the army in 1906.

Chief Geronimo

Geronimo (Chiricahua Apache) (1829–1909), Apache leader, was born along the upper Gila River near present-day Clifton, Arizona. A full-blooded Chiricahua, he fought under Cochise and Mangas Coloradas. Although not a chief by birth, he proved his skill and courage in battle, especially against the Mexicans who had killed his mother, wife, and three children. Because of his great influence, he also came to be regarded as a medicine man.

In 1874, when Geronimo learned that the Chiricahuas were to be relocated from Apache Pass to the San Carlos Reservation, he and his followers escaped across the Mexican border into the Sierra Madre. He raided Mexican settlements and sold the stolen livestock to traders in New Mexico. When he visited the Warm Springs Reservation in New Mexico, Geronimo was arrested and taken to San Carlos where he remained until 1881. After conflict with army troops, he escaped the reservation with Juh, Naiche, Chato, and seventy-four other Apache to the mountains of Mexico. They returned to raid the reservation the following year, after which General George Crook was assigned to the Southwest to hunt down Geronimo and the defiant Apache. With Apache scouts and trackers, they found and attacked Chato's camp, eventually convincing the leaders, including Geronimo, to return to San Carlos.

Geronimo and other leaders left the reservation again with about 150 Apache in May 1885. They were tracked down by Crook's troops in March 1886 and agreed to return, but Geronimo and Naiche, along with twenty-four other Apache, escaped on the way back. General Nelson Miles replaced Crook and he pursued Geronimo and his small band for months. Although he had five thousand soldiers, he could not catch the elusive Geronimo. On September 4, 1886, Geronimo and his followers surrendered for the last time at Canyon de los Embudos, about 65 miles (105 km) south of Apache Pass.

Along with hundreds of other Apache, Geronimo was sent by railroad to prison in Florida. About a year later, some of the Apache, including Geronimo, were moved to Alabama. Many died of tuberculosis and other diseases in the humid climate. Geronimo and the other Chiricahuas were never allowed to return to their homeland. In 1894, they accepted an offer from the Kiowas and Comanches to share their reservation near Fort Sill in present-day Oklahoma. Geronimo farmed there and wrote his memoirs. When he died in 1909, he was still considered a prisoner of war.

This statue by Allan Houser stands outside the Oklahoma Capitol building today.

Allan Houser (Chiricahua Apache) (1914–1994), acclaimed sculptor, was born near Apache, Oklahoma. In the 1960s, he became a charter faculty member of the Institute of American Indian Arts in Santa Fe, New Mexico, where he cast bronze statues and taught until 1975. Thereafter, he devoted himself to creating bronze, stone, and wood sculptures. He was best known for large sculptures, and his work is today included in the collections of the Metropolitan Museum of Art, the Heard Museum, the Denver Art Museum, and the Fine Arts Museum of the University of New Mexico, among others.

Houser received many awards for his work, including the Prix de West Award in 1993 for a bronze sculpture entitled *Smoke Signals*. One of his most famous works, a bronze statue of a Native woman entitled *As Long as the Waters Flow*, today stands in front of the state capitol in Oklahoma City. In 1994, he presented an 11-foot (3.4 m) bronze sculpture to First Lady Hillary Rodham Clinton as a gift from Native Americans to all people.

Lozen (Mimbreno Apache) (ca. 1840–1890), warrior woman and prophetess, sister to Victorio, remains a prominent figure in Apache history. She was a woman of incredible strength, determination, and dedication to her people. She was said to be more of a military strategist and leader than her brother at times. She accompanied Victorio on raids after fleeing the San Carlos Reservation in 1877. Often, in photographs, she is unrecognizable from the other warriors of her tribe. She is described as having a manly appearance, very different from Dahteste. She likewise was rumored to have the ability to read the minds of her enemies and evade capture. Stories tell of her demonstrating great courage and sensitivity to her people, having once journeyed with a mother and her newborn child to the Mescalero Reservation, evading US soldiers along

Lozen, a woman warrior, is seen here among Geronimo's band of warriors, with Dahteste on her right. She is highlighted in green.

the way. She, along with Dahteste, helped negotiate Geronimo's surrender to the US Cavalry. She spent her final days imprisoned at the Mount Vernon Barracks in Alabama, where she died around 1890, most likely from tuberculosis.

Naiche (Natchez, Nachi, Nache) (Chiricahua Apache) (ca. 1857–1921), son of Cochise and grandson of Mangas Coloradas, was a leader during conflicts with US forces in the late 1800s. He was with his father during the Bascom Affair and was briefly held hostage.

His father taught him to remain loyal to his brother Taza. When Taza died unexpectedly of pneumonia in 1876, Naiche, whose name means "the Mischief Maker," led raiding parties. A hereditary chief, Naiche was a close ally of Geronimo in the Apache Wars. In 1879, he resisted relocation on the San Carlos Reservation and fled to Mexico with Geronimo's band. After years of conflict with US military forces, he finally surrendered with Geronimo in 1886. Relocated and imprisoned at Fort Marion, Florida, in 1894, he was moved to Fort Sill in present-day Oklahoma along with other Apache, including Geronimo. Naiche was not permitted to return to his homeland in Arizona until 1913. Eight years later, he died of influenza.

Victorio (Mimbreno Apache) (ca. 1825–1880), leader, was likely born in southern New Mexico. As a young man, Victorio fought under Mangas Coloradas. When the great Mimbreno chief died in 1863, Victorio became a leader of his and other Apache bands. This group, which included Mimbreno, Mogollon, Copper Mine, Chiricahua, and Mescalero, became known as the Ojo Caliente, or Warm Springs, Apache, after the location of their agency in southwestern New Mexico.

During the 1860s and 1870s, the Warm Springs Apache frequently raided in New Mexico and Texas. Victorio offered to stop the attacks if his people were given a permanent reservation. However, he and his followers were forced to move to the San Carlos Reservation where they lived with the Chiricahuas. In 1877, Victorio and about three hundred followers escaped, but most surrendered within a month

at Fort Wingate, New Mexico. Victorio and about eighty warriors hid out in the Mimbres Mountains and occasionally raided settlements in the region. At the beginning of 1879, he attempted to settle at Warm Springs again, but in June he agreed instead to move to the Mescalero Reservation at Tularosa, New Mexico. Indicted on a charge of murder and horse theft, he fled with several warriors and a number of Mescaleros. They attacked a cavalry camp, killing eight soldiers, then went to Mexico. As they wandered into Texas, back into New Mexico, and then into Arizona, they engaged in a series of raids.

While fleeing American soldiers in October 1880, Victorio and his followers were attacked by Mexican and Tarahumara tribes. During the two-day battle of Tres Castillos, about eighty Apache were killed and almost as many women and children were

This Apache warrior's cloak is decorated with pictures of a god and spirits.

taken prisoner. Only about thirty warriors escaped—but not Victorio. He was found among the dead, either killed by a Tarahumara or having taken his own life.

Throughout their history, the Apache people have had varied and courageous leaders, scouts, and rebels. These men and women have added to the story of their bands and live on in memory and in tales such as these. They, along with the men and women before and after them, have helped preserve the Apache way of life and have made the tribe what it is today.

CHRONOLOGY

10,000 BCE First Native peoples come to live in the American Southwest.

1200–1400 CE Athapascan-speaking people (Apache and Navajos) arrive in the Southwest.

1450 Another wave of migration scatters early Athapascan-speaking peoples throughout the Southwest.

1527 Four Spanish explorers from Pánfilo de Narváez's expedition travel into Apache territory.

ca. 1540 Francisco Vásquez de Coronado encounters the Apache during his journey through the Southwest.

1598 Juan de Oñate claims New Mexico as a colony that is divided into governmental districts.

1610 Spain formally claims the entire Southwest, including Apache land, as a colony in the New World.

1600s Wandering Apache bands avoid capture and enslavement by Spanish colonists.

1700s Apache continually war with the Spanish and Mexican invaders.

1821 Mexico wins independence from Spain and takes control of New Mexico, including Apache lands.

1824 The United States establishes the Bureau of Indian Affairs under the Department of War.

1829 Geronimo is born.

1830s Mexico offers a bounty for Native American scalps.

1848 The Mexican War concludes with the Treaty of Guadalupe Hidalgo, which cedes the Southwest, including Apache lands, to the United States.

1850s Forts are built in Apache territory.

1851 Mescalero and Jicarilla Apache sign a peace treaty with James C. Calhoun, governor of New Mexico Territory. After a severe beating, Mangas Coloradas goes on the warpath.

1858 Geronimo, a Chiricahua Apache, discovers that his mother, wife, and children have been murdered by Spanish troops from Mexico.

1861 War again breaks out between the Chiricahua Apache and the United States. Cochise eludes the US

Army and goes on the warpath.

1863 Mangas Coloradas is captured and killed. After his death, Cochise becomes principal chief.

1870 The US government establishes reservations for the Apache.

1871 Settlers massacre more than a hundred Apache, mostly women and children, at Camp Grant.

1871–1872 Apache are assigned to four reservations in the Southwest.

1872 Cochise signs a treaty with General Oliver Howard in which he agrees to end raids against settlers.

1874 Cochise dies of an unknown illness, and the Western Apache are forced onto San Carlos Reservation.

1876 Refusing to live on a reservation, Geronimo flees to Mexico with his small band of Chiricahua Apache.

1876–1886 Geronimo and his band fight in Arizona and Mexico to keep their freedom; Victorio is defeated at Tres Castillos in 1880; Geronimo finally surrenders to the US Army in 1886.

1886–1894 The United States government exiles Apache

bands to Alabama and then Florida, far from their homeland.

1894 Exiled Apache, including Geronimo, are sent as prisoners to Fort Sill near present-day Lawton, Oklahoma.

1909 Geronimo dies at Fort Sill, Oklahoma.

1934 The Indian Reorganization Act recognizes tribal governments, beginning the process of self-government for the Apache.

1940s Apache seek compensation for land that was taken by the United States.

1970 Jicarilla Apache receive $10 million from the Indian Claims Commission.

1982 The Jicarilla Apache win the right to tax minerals extracted from their land in the United States Supreme Court case *Merrion v. Jicarilla Apache Tribe*.

2015 White Mountain Apache Tribe's Annual Fair and Rodeo celebrates its ninetieth year.

GLOSSARY

Apachería The Spanish name for Apache lands. Also sometimes called Grand Apachería.

Athapascan The language family of the Apache and Navajos and many Native peoples of western Canada and Alaska. Also the ancient people from whom these tribes descend.

Bascom Affair The clash between United States soldiers led by Lieutenant George Bascom and Apache leader Cochise and his warriors over the alleged kidnapping of a boy named Mickey Free. The conflict expanded into the Apache Wars.

bear grass A grassy plant used to thatch wickiups.

canyon A deep valley, usually fairly narrow, with steep, rocky walls on either side.

Chiricahua An Apache people now living in New Mexico and Oklahoma.

cradleboard A wooden board used to carry a baby.

Four Corners A common name for the place where the borders of Utah, Colorado, Arizona, and New Mexico come together.

Hactcin Spirit powers; creators of the world in the Jicarilla Apache origin story.

Jicarilla An Apache people now living in New Mexico.

Mescalero An Apache people now living in Arizona; the name refers to the mescal plant, gathered for food.

Ndee The name the Apache use for themselves, meaning "the people." Also N'de and Ndé.

plateau High, flat land.

pone Bread often made without milk or eggs and baked or fried.

shaman A medicine man or woman who led all Apache religious ceremonies.

Western Apache People living in Arizona, including White Mountain Apache, San Carlos Apache, Northern Tonto, and Southern Tonto.

wickiup A dome-shaped shelter made of saplings and brush used by the Apache.

Zuñi A group of people native to western New Mexico and eastern Arizona in the United States.

BIBLIOGRAPHY

Aleshire, Peter. *Warrior Woman: The Story of Lozen, Apache Warrior and Shaman.* New York: St. Martin's Press, 2001.

Alvarez, Alex. *Native America and the Question of Genocide.* Studies in Genocide: Religion, History, and Human Rights. Lanham, MD: Rowman & Littlefield Publishers, 2014.

Bourke, John Gregory. *On the Border with Crook: General George Crook, the American Indian Wars, and Life on the American Frontier.* New York: Skyhorse Publishing, 2014.

Chamberlain, Kathleen P. *Victorio: Apache Warrior and Chief.* The Oklahoma Western Biographies. Norman, OK: University of Oklahoma Press, 2007.

Dunbar-Oritz, Roxanne. *An Indigenous Peoples' History of the United States.* Boston: Beacon Press, 2014.

Editors, Charles River. *The Apache.* Native American Tribes. Seattle, WA: CreateSpace, 2013.

Jacoby, Karl. *Shadows at Dawn: An Apache Massacre and the Violence of History*. Penguin History of American Life. New York: Penguin Group USA, 2008.

Kiser, William S. *Dragoons in Apacheland: Conquest and Resistance in Southern New Mexico, 1846–1861*. Norman, OK: University of Oklahoma Press, 2013.

Leach, Mike, and Buddy Levy. *Geronimo: Leadership Strategies of an American Warrior*. New York: Gallery Books, 2014.

Mauro, Hayes Peter. *The Art of Americanization at the Carlisle Indian School*. Albuquerque, NM: University of New Mexico Press, 2011.

McKanna, Clare V. Jr. *Court-Martial of Apache Kid: Renegade of Renegades*. Lubbock, TX: Texas Tech University Press, 2009.

Mort, Terry. *The Wrath of Cochise: The Bascom Affair and the Origins of the Apache Wars*. New York: Pegasus, 2012.

Page, Jake. *In the Hands of the Great Spirit: The 20,000-Year History of American Indians*. New York: Free Press, 2004.

Reyhner, Jon, and Jeanette Eder. *American Indian Education: A History*. Norman, OK: University of Oklahoma Press, 2006.

Robinson, Sherry. *Apache Voices: Their Stories of Survival as Told to Eve Ball*. Albuquerque, NM: University of New Mexico Press, 2003.

Sánchez, Lynda A. *Apache Legends and Lore of Southern New Mexico: From the Sacred Mountain*. Charleston, SC: The History Press, 2014.

Sweeney, Edwin R., ed. *Cochise: Firsthand Accounts of the Chiricahua Apache Chief*. Norman, OK: University of Oklahoma Press, 2014.

Sweeney, Edwin R. *From Cochise to Geronimo: The Chiricahua Apache 1874-1886*. Norman, OK: University of Oklahoma Press, 2012.

Trafzer, Clifford E., and Jean A. Keller, eds. *Boarding School Blues: Revisiting American Indian Educational Experiences*. Indigenous Education. Lincoln, NE: Bison Books, 2006.

Watt, Robert, and Adam Hook. *Apache Tactics 1830-86*. Oxford, England: Osprey Publishing, 2012.

FURTHER INFORMATION

Want to know more about the Apache Nation? Check out these websites, videos, and organizations.

Websites

Biography of Geronimo

www.biography.com/people/geronimo-9309607

This website gives a detailed history of Geronimo, one of the Apache leaders.

Deming Arts Center

www.demingarts.org

The official website of the Deming Arts Center in Deming, New Mexico, a museum that has featured Apache art, including the exhibit "Celebrating 100 years of Apache Freedom," displayed in April 2015.

Encyclopedia Britannica: Apache

www.britannica.com/EBchecked/topic/29265/Apache

This website describes the history of the Apache tribes.

United States Bureau of Indian Affairs

www.bia.gov

This is the official website of the United States Bureau of Indian Affairs.

White Mountain Culture Center and Museum

www.wmat.nsn.us/wmaculture.html

This website features information about the White Mountain Culture Center and Museum, a place that displays information about the Apache tribe living there, past and present.

Videos

CrashCourse: Westward Expansion

www.youtube.com/watch?v=Q16OZkgSXfM

This video describes the concept of Westward Expansion, how it worked, and who it benefited and harmed.

Into the West: Carlisle Indian Industrial School

www.youtube.com/watch?v=yfRHqWCz3Zw

This clip illustrates what it was like for Native American children to attend an industrial school in the 1800s.

Racing the Past: Voices from the Apache Reservations

www.youtube.com/watch?v=l_L6FdOaOS8

This video shows interviews with young people living on reservations in Arizona today.

Organizations

Apache Business Committee
PO Box 1330
Anadarko, OK 73005
(405) 247-9493
www.apachetribe.org

Apache Tribe of Fort Sill
43187 US Hwy 281
Apache, OK 73006
(580) 588-2298
www.fortsillapache-nsn.gov

Fort McDowell Yavapai Nation
PO Box 17779
Fountain Hills, AZ 85269
(480) 837-5121
www.fmyn.org

Jicarilla Apache Nation
Dulce, NM 87528
(575) 759-3242
www.jicarillaonline.com

Mescalero Apache Tribal Council
108 M376
Mescalero, NM 88340
(575) 464-4494
mescaleroapachetribe.com

San Carlos Apache

PO Box 0

San Carlos, AZ 85550

(928) 475-2361

www.sancarlosapache.com

Tonto Apache Tribal Council

Tonto Apache Reservation #30

Payson, AZ 85541

(928) 474-5000

White Mountain Apache Tribal Council

PO Box 700

Whiteriver, AZ 85941

(928) 338-4346

www.wmat.nsn.us

Yavapai-Apache Community Council

333 W Middle Verde Rd.

Camp Verde, AZ 86322

(928) 567-3649

yavapai-apache.org

INDEX

ABOUT THE AUTHOR

Raymond Bial has published more than eighty books—most of them photography books—during his career. His photo-essays for children include *Corn Belt Harvest*, *Amish Home*, *Frontier Home*, *Shaker Home*, *The Underground Railroad*, *Portrait of a Farm Family*, *With Needle and Thread: A Book About Quilts*, *Mist Over the Mountains: Appalachia and Its People*, *Cajun Home*, and *Where Lincoln Walked*.

As with his other work, Bial's deep feeling for his subjects is evident in both the text and illustrations. He travels to tribal cultural centers, photographing homes, artifacts, and surroundings and learning firsthand about the national lifeways of these peoples.

The emeritus director of a small college library in the Midwest, he lives with his wife and three children in Urbana, Illinois.